101
THANKSGIVING
Blessings

101
THANKSGIVING
Blessings

Vickie Phelps

BARBOUR
PUBLISHING

All scripture quotations are taken from the King James Version of the Bible.

Published by Barbour Publishing, Inc., P.O. Box 719, Uhrichsville, Ohio 44683, www.barbourbooks.com

Our mission is to publish and distribute inspirational products offering exceptional value and biblical encouragement to the masses.

 Member of the
Evangelical Christian
Publishers Association

Printed in the United States of America.

INTRODUCTION

What are you thankful for this Thanksgiving? Food, family, friendship, shelter, love—all of these are important blessings for which to give thanks. But our gratitude can encompass so much more. From sharing coffee with a friend to a rainbow after a storm and good health to beautiful artwork, use the 101 blessings in this book as a way to widen and deepen your thankfulness to the Giver of all good things. Then and only then will you experience true Thanksgiving.

1. THE LOVE OF FAMILY.

And I will bless them that bless thee, and curse him that curseth thee: and in thee shall all families of the earth be blessed.

GENESIS 12:3

2. TRUE FRIENDS WHO ARE THERE REGARDLESS OF CIRCUMSTANCES.

A friend loveth at all times.

PROVERBS 17:17

3. GOD'S WORD, THE BREAD OF LIFE.

It is written, That man shall not live by bread alone, but by every word of God.

LUKE 4:4

4. FREEDOM OF WORSHIP.

I will worship toward thy holy
temple, and praise thy name.

PSALM 138:2

5. Beautiful Music to Enjoy.

Sing unto him a new song;
play skilfully with a loud noise.

Psalm 33:3

6. THE WARMTH OF A FIRE IN WINTER.

I will praise thee, O Lord, with my whole heart; I will shew forth all thy marvellous works.

PSALM 9:1

7. OUR FOREFATHERS WHO PAVED THE WAY FOR US.

Thus saith the LORD, Stand ye in the ways, and see, and ask for the old paths, where is the good way, and walk therein.

JEREMIAH 6:16

8. A MOTHER'S LOVE.

For I was my father's son,
tender and only beloved in the sight
of my mother.

PROVERBS 4:3

9. THE SINGING OF BIRDS.

The flowers appear on the earth;
the time of the singing of birds is
come, and the voice of the turtle is
heard in our land.

SONG OF SOLOMON 2:12

10. RAIN IN DUE SEASON.

*Then I will give you rain in due
season, and the land shall yield her
increase, and the trees of the field
shall yield their fruit.*

LEVITICUS 26:4

11. TWO HANDS TO PERFORM TASKS.

Whatsoever thy hand findeth to do, do it with thy might; for there is no work, nor device, nor knowledge, nor wisdom, in the grave, whither thou goest.

ECCLESIASTES 9:10

12. LAUGHTER TO EXPRESS OUR JOY.

Then was our mouth filled with laughter, and our tongue with singing: then said they among the heathen, The LORD hath done great things for them.

PSALM 126:2

13. THE ACT OF FORGIVENESS.

And be ye kind one to another, tenderhearted, forgiving one another, even as God for Christ's sake hath forgiven you.

EPHESIANS 4:32

14. SPRING FLOWERS.

Thou waterest the ridges thereof abundantly: thou settlest the furrows thereof: thou makest it soft with showers: thou blessest the springing thereof.

PSALM 65:10

15. AUTUMN LEAF COLOR.

To every thing there is a season,
and a time to every purpose under
the heaven.

ECCLESIASTES 3:1

16. THE INSTRUCTION OF A FATHER.

My son, hear the instruction of thy father, and forsake not the law of thy mother: for they shall be an ornament of grace unto thy head.

PROVERBS 1:8–9

17. THE INNOCENCE
OF CHILDREN.

But Jesus said, Suffer little
children, and forbid them not,
to come unto me: for of such
is the kingdom of heaven.

MATTHEW 19:14

18. PEACEFUL SLEEP.

*I will both lay me down in peace,
and sleep: for thou, LORD, only
makest me dwell in safety.*

PSALM 4:8

19. TEARS EXPRESSING OUR JOY OR GRIEF.

They that sow in tears shall reap in joy.

PSALM 126:5

20. A SISTER'S LOVE.

*Charity suffereth long, and is
kind; charity envieth not; charity
vaunteth not itself, is not puffed up.*
1 CORINTHIANS 13:4

21. SUNSHINE AFTER STORMS.

The day is thine, the night also is thine: thou hast prepared the light and the sun.

PSALM 74:16

22. THE ABILITY TO LEARN.

*A wise man will hear, and will
increase learning; and a man of
understanding shall attain unto
wise counsels.*

PROVERBS 1:5

23. KIND WORDS.

*A man hath joy by the answer of
his mouth: and a word spoken in
due season, how good is it!*
                    PROVERBS 15:23

24. THE PURSUIT OF HAPPINESS.

Happy is he that hath the God of Jacob for his help, whose hope is in the LORD his God.

PSALM 146:5

25. LIPS THAT WORSHIP GOD.

*My soul shall be satisfied as with
marrow and fatness; and my mouth
shall praise thee with joyful lips.*

PSALM 63:5

26. EYES TO ENJOY THE WORLD AROUND US.

*Truly the light is sweet, and a
pleasant thing it is for the eyes to
behold the sun.*

ECCLESIASTES 11:7

27. THE WISDOM OF OUR ELDERS.

Likewise, ye younger, submit yourselves unto the elder. Yea, all of you be subject one to another.

1 PETER 5:5

28. FOOD ON OUR TABLE.

And having food and raiment let us be therewith content.

1 TIMOTHY 6:8

29. GOD-GIVEN TALENTS.

But now hath God set the members
every one of them in the body, as it
hath pleased him.

1 CORINTHIANS 12:18

30. A PLACE TO WORSHIP GOD.

I was glad when they said unto me, Let us go into the house of the LORD.

PSALM 122:1

31. THE WARMTH OF SUNSHINE.

From the rising of the sun unto the going down of the same the LORD's name is to be praised.

PSALM 133:13

32. FRESH WATER TO DRINK.

*And ye shall serve the LORD your
God, and he shall bless thy bread,
and thy water.*

Exodus 23:25

33. COOL BREEZES ON A HOT DAY.

He causeth his wind to blow,
and the waters flow.

PSALM 147:18

34. LAUGHTER IN THE MIDST OF SORROW.

*Even in laughter the heart
is sorrowful.*

PROVERBS 14:13

35. COMFORT FROM A GOOD FRIEND.

*Iron sharpeneth iron; so a man
sharpeneth the countenance of his
friend.*

PROVERBS 27:17

36. GOD'S PROMISES.

*The Lord is not slack concerning
his promise, as some men count
slackness; but is longsuffering to
us-ward.*

2 PETER 3:9

37. THE DIVERSITY OF THE FOUR SEASONS.

Thou hast set all the borders of the earth: thou hast made summer and winter.

PSALM 74:17

38. A VOICE TO SING SONGS.

I will be glad and rejoice in thee: I
will sing praise to thy name,
O thou most High.

PSALM 9:2

39. THE BREATH OF LIFE.

And the LORD God formed man of the dust of the ground, and breathed into his nostrils the breath of life; and man became a living soul.

GENESIS 2:7

40. THE LOVE OF A MATE.

*Therefore shall a man leave his
father and his mother, and shall
cleave unto his wife: and they shall
be one flesh.*

GENESIS 2:24

41. CHILDREN IN THE FAMILY.

*Lo, children are an heritage of the
LORD: and the fruit of the womb
is his reward.*

PSALM 127:3

42. GOOD HEALTH.

*Beloved, I wish above all things
that thou mayest prosper and be in
health, even as thy soul prospereth.*

3 JOHN 1:2

43. A GODLY HERITAGE.

*When I call to remembrance the
unfeigned faith that is in thee,
which dwelt first in thy
grandmother Lois, and thy
mother Eunice; and I am
persuaded that in thee also.*
2 TIMOTHY 1:5

44. EARS TO HEAR.

The ear that heareth the reproof of life abideth among the wise.

PROVERBS 15:31

45. COFFEE WITH A FRIEND.

*He that is of a merry heart hath a
continual feast.*

PROVERBS 15:15

46. THE CONFIDENCE OF A FRIEND.

A talebearer revealeth secrets: but he that is of a faithful spirit concealeth the matter.

PROVERBS 11:13

47. TIME SPENT WITH FAMILY.

*Blessed is every one that feareth the
LORD; that walketh in his ways.
Thy wife shall be as a fruitful vine
by the sides of thine house: thy
children like olive plants round
about thy table.*

PSALM 128:1, 3

48. A GODLY MENTOR.

Where no counsel is, the people fall:
but in the multitude of counsellors
there is safety.

PROVERBS 11:14

49. PRODUCTIVE GARDENS.

*Build ye houses, and dwell in
them; and plant gardens,
and eat the fruit of them.*

JEREMIAH 29:5

50. TIME SPENT CONVERSING WITH GOD.

I love them that love me; and those
that seek me early shall find me.

PROVERBS 8:17

51. LETTERS FROM A LOVED ONE.

*Heaviness in the heart of man
maketh it stoop: but a good word
maketh it glad.*

PROVERBS 12:25

52. A REPORT OF GOOD NEWS.

As cold waters to a thirsty soul,
so is good news from a far country.
PROVERBS 25:25

53. INSPIRING, CARING TEACHERS.

Give instruction to a wise man, and he will be yet wiser: teach a just man, and he will increase in learning.

PROVERBS 9:9

54. THE DESIRE FOR AN ABUNDANT LIFE.

I am come that they might have life, and that they might have it more abundantly.

JOHN 10:10

55. HOPE FOR TOMORROW.

For thou art my hope, O Lord
GOD: thou art my trust from my
youth.

PSALM 71:5

56. GOOD BOOKS TO READ.

Whoso loveth instruction loveth
knowledge.

PROVERBS 12:1

57. THE GIFT OF GOD'S GRACE.

For by grace are ye saved through
faith; and that not of yourselves:
it is the gift of God.

EPHESIANS 2:8

58. COURAGE TO PURSUE OUR DREAMS.

*I can do all things through Christ
which strengtheneth me.*

PHILIPPIANS 4:13

59. THE COMFORT OF A BED FOR SLEEPING.

Stand in awe, and sin not:
commune with your own heart
upon your bed, and be still.

PSALM 4:4

60. THE BEAUTY OF THE STARS ON A DARK NIGHT.

When I consider thy heavens, the work of thy fingers, the moon and the stars, which thou hast ordained; what is man, that thou art mindful of him?

PSALM 8:3–4

61. THE COMPANIONSHIP OF ANIMALS.

And out of the ground the LORD God formed every beast of the field, and every fowl of the air; and brought them unto Adam to see what he would call them: and whatsoever Adam called every living creature, that was the name thereof.

GENESIS 2:19

62. THE HARVEST OF A GARDEN.

For thou shalt eat the labour of thine hands: happy shalt thou be, and it shall be well with thee.

PSALM 128:2

63. MODERN TECHNOLOGY.

When the wise is instructed,
he receiveth knowledge.

PROVERBS 21:11

64. REST AFTER HARD WORK.

Six days thou shalt do thy work,
and on the seventh day thou shalt
rest.

EXODUS 23:12

65. PRAYER OFFERED FOR YOU BY A FRIEND.

Confess your faults one to another, and pray one for another, that ye may be healed. The effectual fervent prayer of a righteous man availeth much.

JAMES 5:16

66. BEAUTIFUL ARTWORK.

I will call upon the LORD, who is worthy to be praised.

PSALM 18:3

67. THE SKILL OF A GOOD DOCTOR.

*Many are the afflictions of the
righteous: but the LORD delivereth
him out of them all.*

PSALM 34:19

68. RAINBOWS AFTER A STORM.

And it shall come to pass, when I bring a cloud over the earth, that the bow shall be seen in the cloud.

GENESIS 9:14

69. FRIENDS WITH STRONG SHOULDERS TO LEAN ON.

*Ointment and perfume rejoice the
heart: so doth the sweetness of a
man's friend by hearty counsel.*

PROVERBS 27:9

70. FAMILY HOLIDAY CELEBRATIONS.

Behold, how good and how pleasant it is for brethren to dwell together in unity!

PSALM 133:1

71. AIR-CONDITIONING IN THE SUMMER.

O give thanks unto the LORD; call upon his name: make known his deeds among the people.

PSALM 105:1

72. Mentors who care.

The rich and poor meet together:
the LORD is the maker of them all.

Proverbs 22:2

73. AN UNEXPECTED VALENTINE.

*Beloved, let us love one another:
for love is of God; and every one
that loveth is born of God, and
knoweth God.*

1 JOHN 4:7

74. GOD'S MERCY.

For the LORD is good; his mercy is
everlasting; and his truth endureth
to all generations.

PSALM 100:5

75. INNER JOY THAT MAKES YOU SMILE.

Thou wilt shew me the path of life: in thy presence is fulness of joy; at thy right hand there are pleasures for evermore.

PSALM 16:11

76. EMPLOYMENT.

Whatsoever thy hand findeth to do, do it with thy might.

ECCLESIASTES 9:10

77. THE ABILITY TO LAUGH.

A merry heart doeth good like a medicine.

PROVERBS 17:22

78. THE SHADE OF A BIG TREE.

The shady trees cover him with
their shadow; the willows of the
brook compass him about.

JOB 40:22

79. VICTORY AFTER A BATTLE.

For whatsoever is born of God
overcometh the world: and this is
the victory that overcometh the
world, even our faith.

1 JOHN 5:4

80. STRENGTH TO RUN A RACE.

For by thee I have run through a troop; and by my God have I leaped over a wall.

PSALM 18:29

81. THE SMALL THINGS IN LIFE.

*Bless the LORD, O my soul, and
forget not all his benefits.*

PSALM 103:2

82. SPIRITUAL DIRECTION.

*Blessed is the man that walketh
not in the counsel of the ungodly,
nor standeth in the way of sinners,
nor sitteth in the seat of the
scornful.*

PSALM 1:1

83. A FIELD OF WILDFLOWERS.

*The glory of the LORD shall endure
for ever: the LORD shall rejoice in
his works.*

PSALM 104:31

84. THE MAJESTY OF MOUNTAINS.

As the mountains are round about Jerusalem, so the LORD is round about his people from henceforth even for ever.

PSALM 125:2

85. THE DESIRE TO SMILE.

*Happy is that people, whose God is
the LORD.*

PSALM 144:15

86. TIME TO SMELL THE ROSES.

Be still, and know that I am God.

PSALM 46:10

87. Opportunities to Improve Yourself.

*Hear, ye children, the instruction
of a father, and attend to know
understanding.*

PROVERBS 4:1

88. COMMUNICATION WITH OTHERS.

*Righteous lips are the delight of
kings; and they love him that
speaketh right.*

PROVERBS 16:13

89. COMMON COURTESY FROM OTHERS.

Look not every man on his own things, but every man also on the things of others.

PHILIPPIANS 2:4

90. LEISURE TIME WITH FRIENDS.

*Be kindly affectioned one to
another with brotherly love;
in honour preferring one another.*
ROMANS 12:10

91. THE ABILITY TO PROVIDE FOR YOUR FAMILY.

She looketh well to the ways of her household, and eateth not the bread of idleness.

PROVERBS 31:27

92. WORDS OF WISDOM FROM A FRIEND.

*Hear counsel, and receive
instruction, that thou mayest
be wise in thy latter end.*

PROVERBS 19:20

93. A NEW DAY.

This is the day which the LORD hath made; we will rejoice and be glad in it.

PSALM 118:24

94. BEAUTIFUL POETRY.

The Lord gave the word:
great was the company of
those that published it.

PSALM 68:11

95. COURAGE WHEN NEEDED.

Be strong and of a good courage,
fear not, nor be afraid of them:
for the LORD thy God, he it is
that doth go with thee; he will
not fail thee, nor forsake thee.

DEUTERONOMY 31:6

96. CONTENTMENT.

*But godliness with contentment is
great gain.*

1 TIMOTHY 6:6

97. A BEAUTIFUL SUNSET.

*He appointed the moon for seasons:
the sun knoweth his going down.*

PSALM 104:19

98. A PHONE CALL FROM AN OLD FRIEND OR RELATIVE.

Pleasant words are as an honeycomb, sweet to the soul, and health to the bones.

PROVERBS 16:24

99. EARLY MORNING SOLITUDE WITH GOD.

My meditation of him shall be sweet: I will be glad in the LORD.
PSALM 104:34